Reaching for the Prize

Reaching for the Prize

by
John MacArthur, Jr.

"GRACE TO YOU"
P.O. Box 4000
Panorama City, CA   91412

ISBN: 0-8024-5369-4

1 2 3 4 5 6 Printing/LC/Year 94 93 92 91 90

Printed in the United States of America

Contents

These Bible studies are taken from messages delivered by Pastor-Teacher John MacArthur, Jr., at Grace Community Church in Panorama City, California. These messages have been combined into a 4-tape album titled *Reaching for the Prize*. You may purchase this series either in an attractive vinyl cassette album or as individual cassettes. To purchase these tapes, request the album *Reaching for the Prize*, or ask for the tapes by their individual GC numbers. Please consult the current price list; then, send your order, making your check payable to:

The Master's Communication
P.O. Box 4000
Panorama City, CA 91412

Or call the following toll-free number:
1-800-55-GRACE

1
Reaching for the Prize—Introduction

Outline

Introduction
A. The Context of Pursuing the Prize
B. The Reasons for Pursuing the Prize

Lesson
 I. An Awareness of Need (v. 12*a*)
    A. For More Knowledge
    B. For Practical Righteousness
    C. For More Power
    D. For Better Fellowship
    E. For Glorification
 II. Maximum Effort (v. 12*b*)
    A. The Pursuit
    B. The Prize
III. Concentration (v. 13)
    A. Paul Did Only One Thing
        1. By forgetting the past
        2. By looking ahead
    B. Paul Wanted Only One Thing for Others
 IV. Spiritual Motivation (v. 14)
  V. Divine Revelation (v. 15)
 VI. Consistency (v. 16)
    A. Through the Word
    B. Through Prayer
    C. Through Following an Example
    D. Through Trials

Conclusion

Introduction

In Philippians 3:12-16 Paul says, "Not that I have already obtained it, or have already become perfect, but I press on in order that I may lay hold of that for which also I was laid hold of by Christ Jesus. Brethren, I do not regard myself as having laid hold of it yet; but one thing I do: forgetting what lies behind and reaching forward to what lies ahead, I press on toward the goal for the prize of the upward call of God in Christ Jesus. Let us therefore, as many as are perfect, have this attitude; and if in anything you have a different attitude, God will reveal that also to you; however, let us keep living by that same standard to which we have attained."

Verse 14 is the heart of that passage: "I press on toward the goal for the prize of the upward call of God in Christ Jesus." Paul's theme was reaching for the prize, so he used the analogy of a runner to describe the Christian's spiritual growth.

A. The Context of Pursuing the Prize

   Paul has just described his conversion in verses 4-11. He said he had put aside all he had considered precious (vv. 4-7) to embrace Christ. Verses 8-11 tell us what he gained: knowledge, righteousness, power, fellowship, and glory. Yet even though he received those tremendous spiritual benefits, he was not perfect. In fact, his primary purpose in writing verses 12-16 seems to have been to disclaim spiritual perfection. He didn't want his readers to think that the beginning for him was also the end—that he was instantaneously made perfect when he came to Christ and therefore had nothing more to pursue. It is possible that Judaizers had been telling the Philippians that spiritual perfection was available through circumcision and obedience to the law. Similarly, the Gnostics taught that spiritual perfection could be reached through a supposed higher knowledge.

   Paul rebukes those potential false teachers in verse 12 by reminding his readers that he had not arrived spiritually. Because he still possessed his unredeemed flesh, he remained a temptable sinner. According to Paul, the believer must first realize he is not perfect and then make perfection his goal in life. We must follow Peter's command to "grow in the grace and knowledge of our Lord and Savior Jesus Christ" (2 Pet. 3:18). Though we receive knowledge, righteousness, power, fellowship, and glory in Christ, we are still involved in the growth process. We must pursue the goal and press toward the mark.

B. The Reasons for Pursuing the Prize

Since we as Christians are already entitled to heaven and will attain perfection one day in the presence of God, why should we bother to grow spiritually? In one sense that question is irrelevant because one who is a new creation in Christ will have a desire to grow. We are born into God's family with a hunger and longing for growth. But beyond that there are many important reasons for a believer to run the race and pursue the prize.

1. It glorifies God.

2. It verifies salvation. Outward change demonstrates that true change has occurred on the inside.

3. It is a good testimony. Spiritual growth puts the truth of God on display in our lives for others to see (Titus 2:10).

4. It provides assurance. When we progress spiritually, we see that God is at work in our lives, and that helps us to be "certain about His calling and choosing [us]" (2 Pet. 1:10).

5. It spares us unnecessary sorrow. Lack of growth toward godliness brings only pain and sorrow to the believer.

6. It protects the cause of Christ from reproach.

7. It makes the believer useful for ministering to the church.

Paul vs. Perfectionism

In his disclaimer to the Philippians, Paul left a message to all generations: that perfection in this life is a goal, not an achievement. It's something we pursue but will never attain in this life. Philippians

3:12-16 delivers a death blow to the false doctrine of perfectionism, which teaches that a believer can become sinless in this life. Historically those holding to that doctrine have taught that there is some point following conversion when the believer's sin nature is eradicated. Perfectionism finds its roots in Pelagianism and Arminianism. It was articulated by John Wesley in the eighteenth century and has become a traditional tenet of Wesleyan theology.

Paul denied perfectionism by calling us to pursue a prize that can only be fully obtained in heaven. He confessed that he himself had not reached perfection—and Philippians was written almost thirty years after his conversion! The apostle Paul was perhaps the most committed Christian who ever lived. If after thirty years he wasn't perfect, certainly none of us should claim to be.

Lesson

Philippians 3:12-16 calls us to reach for the prize of spiritual perfection. We are to give our whole lives to that pursuit, and the following six principles will aid us in doing so.

I. AN AWARENESS OF NEED (v. 12*a*)

"Not that I have already obtained it, or have already become perfect."

We are not yet what we should be, what we can be, or what we will be when we see the Lord. Our spiritual race begins with a sense of dissatisfaction. Paul started his race with the awareness that he had not arrived.

I personally can echo Paul's testimony. After many years of walking with the Lord and being involved in ministry, I am still acutely aware that I am not what I ought to be. Like every other believer, I am still in the process of growth. F. B. Meyer wisely observed that "self-dissatisfaction lies at the root of our noblest achievements" (*The Epistle to the Philippians: A Devotional Commentary* [Grand Rapids: Baker, 1952], p. 175). People who become content with where they are spiritually have reached a dangerous point. They are probably insensitive to sin and will tend to defend themselves when they should admit their weakness and seek help.

Spiritual growth begins like any race—the runner must realize there is a course to run, and his all-consuming goal should be to finish. Paul's goal was to "become perfect," and he realized he hadn't reached that.

A. For More Knowledge

Even though Paul knew Christ deeply, in 1 Corinthians 13:12 he says, "Now I know in part, but then [when I see God face to face] I shall know fully."

B. For Practical Righteousness

Even though Paul had the legal righteousness of Christ because of his faith, he needed to cultivate practical righteousness. In 2 Corinthians 7:1 he says, "Let us cleanse ourselves from all defilement of flesh and spirit, perfecting holiness in the fear of God."

C. For More Power

Even though Paul had received "the power of His resurrection" (Phil. 3:10), he still needed to know more of Christ's power. When he entreated God to remove the thorn in his flesh, God said, "My grace is sufficient for you, for power is perfected in weakness" (2 Cor. 12:9). Therefore Paul said, "I will rather boast about my weaknesses, that the power of Christ may dwell in me."

D. For Better Fellowship

Paul said that in our fellowship with God we all need the help of the Holy Spirit, who "helps our weakness; for we do not know how to pray as we should, but the Spirit Himself intercedes for us with groanings too deep for words" (Rom. 8:26).

E. For Glorification

Although Paul had the indwelling Spirit, he was waiting for the full glory of Christ, who will "transform the body of our humble state into conformity with the body of His glory" (Phil. 3:21).

We must start our pursuit the same way Paul did—with the awareness that we have a lot of learning and growing to do. We must never be satisfied with our present condition but should pursue the prize with all our might.

II. MAXIMUM EFFORT (v. 12*b*)

"I press on in order that I may lay hold of that for which also I was laid hold of by Christ Jesus."

A. The Pursuit

The Greek word translated "press on" (*diōkō*) was used of a sprinter and speaks of an aggressive, energetic endeavor. Paul was running with all his might. He expresses no quietism or "let go and let God" theology in this verse. Rather, we see a man straining every spiritual muscle to win the prize (cf. 1 Cor. 9:24-27). That same man said we're to "fight the good fight of faith" (1 Tim. 6:12; cf. 2 Tim. 4:7). Similarly Hebrews 12:1 says, "Let us also lay aside every encumbrance, and the sin which so easily entangles us, and let us run with endurance the race that is set before us." Running the race takes maximum effort using the means of grace God has provided for us.

B. The Prize

What was Paul pursuing? He identified the prize as "that for which I also was laid hold of by Christ Jesus" (Phil. 3:12). Paul wanted to fulfill God's purpose for every believer, which is clearly defined in Romans 8:29: "Whom He foreknew, He also predestined to become conformed to the image of His Son." Second Thessalonians 2:14 says, "It was for this He called you through our gospel, that you may gain the glory of our Lord Jesus Christ." Our lifelong pursuit is to be like Christ. Comparing ourselves to Him will keep us from thinking we have attained that goal.

Becoming like Christ is a worthy goal that requires a lifetime commitment. We must run for that prize with maximum effort.

III. CONCENTRATION (v. 13)

"Brethren, I do not regard myself as having laid hold of it yet; but one thing I do: forgetting what lies behind and reaching forward to what lies ahead."

An athlete running a race must fix his eyes on something ahead of himself. He can't watch his feet or he'll fall on his face. He can't be distracted by watching the other runners. He must focus on the goal straight ahead. Likewise the Christian must concentrate on attaining the goal of Christlikeness.

A. Paul Did Only One Thing

After repeating his disclaimer of perfection, Paul revealed his amazing level of concentration. He had one purpose in life: pressing on "for the prize of the upward call of God in Christ Jesus" (v. 14). That's what made him such a great man.

Paul's remarkable concentration was the result of two things: "Forgetting what lies behind and reaching forward to what lies ahead" (v. 13).

1. By forgetting the past

What does "what lies behind" refer to? Everything in the past, both good and bad. We must refuse to dwell on our virtuous deeds and achievements in ministry, as well as our sins and failures. Why? Because the past has nothing to do with what we're doing right now. We cannot evaluate our usefulness by our past victories, nor should we be debilitated by our past sins and failures. Unfortunately, many Christians are so distracted by the past that they don't make any current progress in the race. Some think that because they taught a Bible study or led someone to the Lord in the past, they don't need to minister now. Others are hung up on guilt from the past, thinking their mistakes were so bad that God can't forgive or use them.

2. By looking ahead

The Greek word translated "reaching forward" (*epek-teinō*) pictures a runner stretching every muscle to reach the goal before him. To do so he must forget the past and concentrate only on the goal ahead. Do you have that kind of concentration in your desire to become like Christ?

B. Paul Wanted Only One Thing for Others

Perfection in Christ was always Paul's goal for those he ministered to.

1. Colossians 1:28—"We proclaim Him, admonishing every man and teaching every man with all wisdom, that we may present every man complete in Christ."

2. Ephesians 4:13—"Until we all attain to the unity of the faith, and of the knowledge of the Son of God, to a mature man, to the measure of the stature which belongs to the fullness of Christ."

3. Galatians 4:19—"My children . . . I am again in labor until Christ is formed in you."

4. 2 Corinthians 13:11—Paul commanded the Corinthians to "be made complete."

5. Colossians 4:12—Paul joined Epaphras, who was "always laboring earnestly for you in his prayers, that you may stand perfect."

To effectively pursue the prize, we must concentrate on becoming like Christ.

IV. SPIRITUAL MOTIVATION (v. 14)

"I press on toward the goal for the prize of the upward call of God in Christ Jesus."

Paul's goal was to be like Christ, and he would receive his reward when God's upward call came. We will not reach the goal of Christlikeness in this life, but we will receive it instantly in the next. First John 3:2 says, "It has not appeared as yet what we shall be. We know that, when He appears, we shall be like Him, because we shall see Him just as He is."

The upward call of God is our motivation to run the race. We should live in light of being called out of this world at any time into the presence of God, where we will receive an eternal reward. We were vile, godless sinners on our way to hell when God sovereignly chose us for salvation that He might eternally make us like His own Son. What grace! What motivation to reach for the goal! Paul lived with that hope in mind. At the end of his ministry he wrote, "I have finished the course. . . . In the future there is laid up for me the crown of righteousness, which the Lord, the righteous judge, will award to me on that day" (2 Tim. 4:7-8).

V. DIVINE REVELATION (v. 15)

"Let us, therefore, as many as are perfect, have this attitude; and if in anything you have a different attitude, God will reveal that also to you."

What did Paul mean by saying, "As many as are perfect"? Since the preceding verses make clear that he wasn't talking about practical perfection, I believe he was talking about positional perfection. Since we as Christians are perfect in God's sight, we should strive for perfection in our daily lives. I think Paul may have used the word "perfect" somewhat sarcastically in reference to those who thought they had reached perfection. It was his way of saying that the only perfection possible in this life is that which we gain through our position in Christ.

Paul wanted all the Philippians to have the same attitude of pursuing the prize, but he knew some would not. Unfortunately, in every church some are preoccupied with the past and content with where they are. Instead of recognizing their need, they spend their lives trying to justify the level they've attained. Others go to the extreme of believing they can live any way they want, like those described in verses 17-21.

Paul said to such people, "If in anything you have a different attitude, God will reveal that also to you." He left them to God. If they were going to get the message, they would have to get it from Him. I pour my heart out in my messages, saying all I can say, but I realize that some people will go on living un-committed lives. When you reach that point with someone you're ministering to, pray, "Lord, I'm not getting through. Please reveal Yourself to this person."

The Greek word translated "reveal" (*apokaluptō*) means "to un-cover or unveil." Paul knew the Lord would reveal the truth to them, perhaps through chastening, as He often does (Heb. 12:5-11). In pursuing the prize we all need to depend on divine resources. There will be times in the race when we don't have the proper attitude, and God will have to reveal that to us so that we can move on.

VI. CONSISTENCY (v. 16)

"Let us keep living by that same standard to which we have at-tained."

You can't win a race with intermittent effort. Christlikeness is an ongoing pursuit. The Greek verb translated "keep living" speaks of walking in line. So Paul was saying, "Stay in line spiritually. Keep moving from where you are by the same principles that got you there." That complements Paul's meta-phor of a runner. In the midst of a race, the runner must stay in his lane and keep up the same effort until he reaches the finish.

A. Through the Word

First Peter 2:2 says, "Like newborn babes, long for the pure milk of the word, that by it you may grow." Constantly reading and studying Scripture will keep us on track.

B. Through Prayer

In 1 Thessalonians 3:10 Paul says, "We night and day keep praying most earnestly that we may see your face, and may complete what is lacking in your faith." Paul saw the ne-cessity of prayer in helping believers become complete.

C. Through Following an Example

In Philippians 3:17 Paul says, "Brethren, join in following my example, and observe those who walk according to the pattern you have in us." Paul said we should pattern our lives after godly people. A spiritual mentor can help us pursue the prize consistently.

D. Through Trials

First Peter 5:10 says, "After you have suffered for a little while, the God of all grace, who called you to His eternal glory in Christ, will Himself perfect, confirm, strengthen and establish you." God brings trials into our lives to push us toward the goal of perfection. James 1:3-4 says, "The testing of your faith produces endurance . . . that you may be perfect and complete, lacking in nothing."

Conclusion

Are you reaching for the prize? Are you growing? Or are you standing in one place looking backward and defending yourself? Perhaps you need to refresh your commitment to run the race. If you don't know Jesus Christ, then start the race by receiving Him as Lord and Savior. If you do know Him but have not been growing spiritually, ask God to forgive you and help you move toward perfection. May we all be committed to the goal of becoming as much like Christ as we can until we see Him.

Focusing on the Facts

1. What is Paul's theme in Philippians 3:12-16? What analogy does he use to discuss it (see p. 8)?
2. What had Paul gained in Christ (Phil. 3:8-11; see p. 8)?
3. What seems to have been Paul's primary purpose in writing Philippians 3:12-16 (see p. 8)?
4. List some reasons Christians should desire to grow spiritually (see p. 9).
5. Did Paul agree with the teaching of perfectionism? Why or why not (see pp. 9-10)?
6. Our spiritual race starts with a sense of _____ (see p. 10).
7. What does the Greek word translated "press on" mean (see p. 12)?

8. What is God's purpose for every believer (Rom. 8:29; see p. 12)?
9. What one thing did Paul do (Phil. 3:13; see pp. 13-14)?
10. What are several verses that show that perfection in Christ was Paul's priority for those he ministered to (see p. 14)?
11. What was Paul's goal in running the race? What was his eventual reward (see pp. 14-15)?
12. In verse 15 Paul was talking about _____ perfection (see p. 15).
13. Name four things that will help us maintain consistency in running the race (see pp. 16-17).

Pondering the Principles

1. Encumbrances and obstacles slow a runner considerably in any race. So it is with spiritual growth. Hebrews 12:1 says, "Let us . . . lay aside every encumbrance, and the sin which so easily entangles us, and let us run with endurance the race that is set before us." Examine your life to determine what may be holding you back in your spiritual race. It may be possessions or pleasures that are not wrong in themselves but perhaps distract you from spiritual things. Also, ask God to reveal any sin in your life and then confess and forsake it.

2. A tremendous amount of self-discipline is necessary to run a race effectively. Paul said, "Do you not know that those who run in a race all run, but only one receives the prize? Run in such a way that you may win. And everyone who competes in the games exercises self-control in all things. . . . Therefore I run in such a way, as not without aim" (1 Cor. 9:24-26). Do you approach your Christian life with the same intensity as an athlete training for an event? Write down some ways in which you can "train yourself to be godly. For physical training is of some value, but godliness has value for all things, holding promise for both the present life and the life to come" (1 Tim. 4:7-8; NIV*).

* New International Version.

2
Following Godly Examples

Outline

Introduction and Review
A. Understanding Our Goal
B. Accomplishing Our Goal
    1. The objective element
    2. The subjective element
    3. The illustration
        a) Paul's testimony
        b) Paul's teaching

Lesson
  I. The Example of Paul
    A. He Was Not Perfect
    B. He Was an Excellent Example
 II. The Example of Others
    A. The Importance of Godly Leaders
    B. The Failure of Today's Leaders

Conclusion

Introduction and Review

Philippians 3:17-21 says, "Brethren, join in following my example, and observe those who walk according to the pattern you have in us. For many walk, of whom I often told you, and now tell you even weeping, that they are enemies of the cross of Christ, whose end is destruction, whose god is their appetite, and whose glory is in their shame, who set their minds on earthly things. For our citizenship is in heaven, from which also we eagerly wait for a Savior,

19

the Lord Jesus Christ; who will transform the body of our humble state into conformity with the body of His glory, by the exertion of the power that He has even to subject all things to Himself."

That passage continues Paul's theme of pursuing the prize. He said in the previous verses that the goal of the Christian life is to become like Jesus Christ. That is a basic truth we need to be reminded of today. Our complex Christian culture has so many seminars, formulas, and theological viewpoints that I fear we sometimes lose sight of what is most important.

A. Understanding Our Goal

The Christian life is simply the process of pursuing Christ's likeness, theologically described as sanctification. Jesus said, "Follow Me," and that simple command has not been replaced or improved upon. Following Christ involves learning from Him so that we can be like Him (Luke 6:40). First John 2:6 says, "The one who says he abides in [Christ] ought himself to walk in the same manner as He walked." Paul wrote to the Galatians, "I am again in labor until Christ is formed in you" (Gal. 4:19). He also told the Corinthians, "Be imitators of me, just as I also am of Christ" (1 Cor. 11:1). Romans 8:29 says God saved us so that we can "become conformed to the image of His Son."

In Philippians 3:12-14 Paul says, "Not that I have already obtained it, or have already become perfect, but I press on in order that I may lay hold of that for which also I was laid hold of by Christ Jesus. Brethren, I do not regard myself as having laid hold of it yet; but one thing I do: forgetting what lies behind and reaching forward to what lies ahead, I press on toward the goal for the prize of the upward call of God in Christ Jesus." By saying "one thing I do," Paul reduced the Christian life to its lowest common denominator—the goal of Christlikeness. We never reach that goal in this life, but God will give it to us as a reward in the life to come. Our goal here is our prize there.

Paul was not a perfectionist. He didn't teach that the believer could reach a point in his life where he was no longer capable of sinning. That certainly was not Paul's experience (Rom. 7). So his one pursuit was to become more and more like Christ. Someone may say, "What about the priority of glorifying God or evangelizing the lost?" Being like Christ glorifies God, and if we are like Christ we will reach out to others. After all, He came "to seek and to save that which was lost" (Luke 19:10). All that is needed in the Christian life will flow out of a pursuit of Christlikeness.

B. Accomplishing Our Goal

Once we understand that our primary pursuit is Christlikeness, we must learn how to accomplish that goal.

1. The objective element

    To become more like Christ we need to know the Word of God. We need to know how Christ lived when He was on earth, and the only place to learn that is the Scriptures, which are the revelation of Christ. The Old Testament sets the scene for Him, creates the need for Him, and predicts His coming. The gospels record His arrival. The book of Acts tells us the immediate impact of His ministry. The epistles delineate the significance of His life and ministry. And Revelation tells us about His future return and judgment of the earth.

    Christ is the focus of the entire Bible, and we need to study it to know what He is like. Too often we study the Bible for the sake of theological arguments or to answer someone's questions. Those things are important, but the main point of Bible study is to know more about Christ so that we can be like Him.

2. The subjective element

    The subjective element in becoming more like Christ is the work of the Holy Spirit. Second Corinthians 3:18 says that as we gaze at the glory of our Lord, we "are being transformed into the same image from glory to glory, just as from the Lord, the Spirit." The Spirit-filled believer will progress toward the goal of Christlikeness because that is the Spirit's work.

Becoming like Christ through the Word and the Spirit is the bottom line of the Christian life.

3. The illustration

   a) Paul's testimony

   Philippians 3:4-6 shows that Paul had a complex life
   before he became a Christian. He was trying to keep
   all the laws and traditions of Judaism. He was trying
   to accomplish various works that he hoped would be
   credited to his account. But in all his pursuits, he was
   seeking something he couldn't find. Then on the Da-
   mascus Road he was confronted by the living Christ
   and realized that Christ was everything. In Philippians 3:7-8 Paul says, "Whatever things were gain to
   me, those things I have counted as loss for the sake of
   Christ. More than that, I count all things to be loss in
   view of the surpassing value of knowing Christ Jesus
   my Lord, for whom I have suffered the loss of all
   things, and count them but rubbish in order that I
   may gain Christ." When Paul met Christ, he realized
   everything in his asset column was a liability. He
   found that Christ was all he needed.

   b) Paul's teaching

   Paul told the Colossians that "in [Christ] are hidden
   all the treasures of wisdom and knowledge" (Col.
   2:3). So the more we know about Christ, the more
   wisdom and knowledge we have. That's why Colossians 2:6 says, "As you therefore have received Christ
   Jesus the Lord, so walk in Him." We're to pattern our
   lives after Christ, "for in Him all the fulness of Deity
   dwells in bodily form, and in Him [we] have been
   made complete" (Col. 2:9-10).

When you read the Word of God, let it speak to you of
Christ and reveal His glory to you. As you yield yourself to
the Spirit of God in obedience, let it be with the desire to be
molded into the image of Christ.

Lesson

In Philippians 3:15-16 Paul exhorts his readers to press toward the goal as he was: "Let us therefore, as many as are perfect, have this attitude; and if in anything you have a different attitude, God will reveal that also to you; however, let us keep living by that same standard to which we have attained." In verses 17-21 we find three practical elements in our pursuit of Christlikeness: following after examples, fleeing from enemies, and focusing on expectations. The first is found in verse 17, where Paul says, "Brethren, join in following my example and observe those who walk according to the pattern you have in us."

I. THE EXAMPLE OF PAUL

A. He Was Not Perfect

Paul was not putting himself on a pedestal of perfection; he was not saying, "I'm perfect—be like me." Rather, he was saying, "I'm imperfect, but follow the way I move toward perfection." Verses 12-16 make clear that Paul had not arrived at perfection, and the rest of the New Testament confirms that.

1. 2 Corinthians 12:7—Apparently Paul was prone to pride, since he said, "To keep me from exalting myself, there was given me a thorn in the flesh, a messenger of Satan to buffet me—to keep me from exalting myself!"

2. Acts 23:3-5—Paul spoke more harshly than he should have to the High Priest when he was being tried.

3. 1 Timothy 1:15—Paul wrote, "Christ Jesus came into the world to save sinners, among whom I am foremost of all." If he were an advocate of perfectionism, he would not have used the present tense. He would have said, "I was the foremost sinner."

4. 1 John 1:8—"If we say that we have no sin, we are deceiving ourselves" (cf. v. 10).

Thus, Paul had not reached sinless perfection. He experienced no alleged second work of grace that rendered him incapable of sin. He was saying, "I have problems with the flesh as well, but follow my example in pursuing the goal."

A Truly Helpful Mountain Guide

If Paul had become perfect, he wouldn't have been an effective example. Since we are imperfect, we need the example of someone who also is imperfect but knows how to deal with imperfection. Let me give you an illustration. Suppose I decide to embark on a dangerous mountain-climbing expedition. A helicopter drops a leader on the top of the mountain, and he looks down at me and says, "This is the top. Just climb up here; this is where you want to be." He would not be as much help as someone climbing the path ahead of me, saying, "Follow me. I know the way up."

Christ shows us the goal we need to achieve, but we also need someone to model the process of reaching that goal. Only by overcoming sin can we become more like Christ, so we have to follow someone who is battling to overcome sin. A godly human example can show us how to deal with all the products of our fallen flesh—our disappointments, trials, temptations, and failures.

B. He Was an Excellent Example

Paul said, "Join in following my example" (Phil. 3:17). The Greek text literally says, "Be fellow imitators (*summimētai*) of me." We get the word *mimic* from this Greek term. Paul was calling the Philippians collectively to follow the way he lived.

There's no better historical example of a Christian than the apostle Paul. He's a dominant figure in the New Testament (he wrote thirteen of the epistles), so we can conclude God wants us to pattern our lives after him. Paul is a model of virtue, worship, service, patience, endurance through suffering, victory over temptation, and managing possessions and relationships. He shows us how a godly man deals with

24

his fallenness—something Christ could never do because He was sinless (Heb. 4:15). Paul's life is a marvelous pattern for ours. That's why he told the Corinthians, "Be imitators of me" (1 Cor. 11:1). He also commended the Thessalonians, saying, "You also became imitators of us and of the Lord" (1 Thess. 1:6). Paul is my own personal example in ministry. I look at how he handled situations and try to respond the way he did.

II. THE EXAMPLE OF OTHERS

Paul went beyond simply calling people to follow him. In Philippians 3:17 he adds, "And observe those who walk according to the pattern you have in us." The Greek word translated "observe" speaks of fixing your gaze on something. We're to focus on godly examples. The word *us* at the end of the verse is an illustration of Paul's humility. He certainly cannot be accused of personal aggrandizement.

A. The Importance of Godly Leaders

In telling the Philippians to observe spiritual examples, Paul probably had Timothy and Epaphroditus in mind. He mentioned both earlier in the book (2:19-30). However, his point carries over to us today. We can always follow Paul's example because it is in print. But that alone is not sufficient—we need flesh-and-blood examples as well. We need to see Christianity lived out before us. The Greek word translated "walk" in Philippians 3:17 refers to daily conduct. We don't have Timothy or Epaphroditus with us today, but we do have godly pastors and elders, who have the responsibility of presenting an example we can follow.

Godly leaders are vital to the church. Paul told Timothy, "In speech, conduct, love, faith and purity, show yourself an example of those who believe" (1 Tim. 4:12). A spiritual leader must have an exemplary life because he is to show others the path. People can see perfection in Christ and can read about Paul, but they also need someone they can watch and talk to. They need to see virtue, humility, unselfish service, a willingness to suffer, devotion to Christ, courage, and spiritual growth in the life of someone close to them. A great burden on my heart is that pastors and elders in every church be the kind of examples God commands them to be. It is extremely important to teach the truth, but it is equally important for that teaching to be undergirded by a virtuous life.

B. The Failure of Today's Leaders

Church history may record ours as the era of disastrous collapse within the leadership of the church. The standards for leadership have been lowered, and many thousands have tragically lost their way.

Where are the Timothys and Epaphrodituses of today? Where are the holy men? Where are the truthful men? Where are the humble, unselfish models of virtue? Where are the examples of victory over temptation? Where are those who show us how to pray and overcome trials or adversity? We ought to have leaders who can honestly say, "Don't just listen to me, but imitate me. Examine my life as closely as you want and follow my pattern."

We are to follow the recorded example of Paul and the living example of godly leaders as our pattern for Christlikeness. Unfortunately, that simple construct has been almost hopelessly skewed today. Our goal and pattern is still to be like Christ, but the interpretation of Scripture has been so blurred in our day that many aren't sure what He is like anymore. Today the church tolerates almost any view about anything, and preaching that is distinct and clear is viewed as offensive. The misunderstanding and misrepresentation of the Holy Spirit's ministry has hindered His work of bringing about Christlikeness. The blurry interpretation of Scripture also keeps us from understanding Paul and following his example. And many of the people in spiritual leadership are anything but patterns we should follow.

Conclusion

We have a sick and distorted church because we've lost sight of Christ, His Word, and the Spirit. We've lost sight of our clear pattern for growth in the life of the apostle Paul. And we have tolerated a lower standard for leadership than the Bible allows. The essence of Christianity is becoming more like Christ. Matters such as right relationships, service, and evangelism will be taken care of if we just pursue that one holy goal.

Focusing on the Facts

1. What is the goal of the Christian life (see p. 20)?
2. What does following Christ involve (Luke 6:40; see p. 20)?
3. What is the Christian's reward in the life to come (see p. 20)?
4. What is the main point of Bible study (see p. 21)?
5. What are hidden in Christ (Col. 2:3; see p. 22)?
6. Give some examples from the New Testament that show Paul was not perfect (see pp. 23-24).
7. What can we conclude from the fact that Paul is such a dominant figure in the New Testament (see p. 24)?
8. What does the word translated "walk" in Philippians 3:17 refer to (see p. 25)?
9. It is extremely important that teaching be undergirded by a _____ _____ (see p. 26).
10. Explain how the modern church has skewed the simple construct for pursuing Christlikeness (see p. 26).

Pondering the Principles

1. Charles Sheldon's famous novel *In His Steps* has helped many Christians understand the priority of Christlikeness. The simple premise of the book is found in the early chapters, when Henry Maxwell issues this challenge to his congregation: "I want volunteers from the First Church who will pledge themselves, earnestly and honestly for an entire year, not to do anything without first asking the question, 'What would Jesus do?'" ([Springdale: Whitaker House, n.d.], p. 27). A number of men and women responded, and the town was never the same again. Are you willing to take Rev. Maxwell's challenge? How would your life change if you were constantly asking, "What would Jesus do?"

2. Scripture presents a high standard for spiritual leadership. Consider the biblical requirements for an elder in 1 Timothy 3:2-7: he "must be above reproach, the husband of one wife, temperate, prudent, respectable, hospitable, able to teach, not addicted to wine or pugnacious, but gentle, uncontentious, free from

the love of money. He must be one who manages his own household well, keeping his children under control with all dignity . . . and not a new convert, lest he become conceited and fall into the condemnation incurred by the devil. And he must have a good reputation with those outside the church, so that he may not fall into reproach and the snare of the devil." If you are in a position of leadership, does your life meet the requirements in that passage? If you are not in leadership, do you desire to be? Paul told Timothy that it's a good thing to desire the office of an overseer. (v. 1). Just be sure that your life matches up with your desires.

3
Fleeing from Enemies

Outline

Introduction and Review
A. The Goal of the Christian Life
B. The Barrier of Humanistic Psychology
    1. Its effect on the gospel
    2. Its effect on sanctification

Lesson
I. Warning About the Enemies of the Cross (v. 18)
    A. They Are Not Readily Apparent
    B. They Are Cause for Great Concern
II. Describing the Enemies of the Cross (v. 19)
    A. They May Have Been Jews
        1. Contemporary parallels
          a) Roman Catholicism
          b) The Worldwide Church of God
        2. The description as it would relate to the Judaizers
          a) Their doom
          b) Their deity
          c) Their disgrace
          d) Their disposition
    B. They May Have Been Gentiles
        1. Contemporary parallels
        2. The description as it would relate to the Gnostics
          a) Their doom
          b) Their deity
          c) Their disgrace
          d) Their disposition

Conclusion

Introduction and Review

A. The Goal of the Christian Life

Philippians 3:18-19 continues the theme of pursuing the prize. Prior to those verses Paul said, "I press on toward the goal for the prize of the upward call of God in Christ Jesus" (v. 14). We have noted that the prize and the goal are the same—becoming like Christ. That was the singular focus of Paul's life. He said, "I count all things to be loss . . . that I may gain Christ" (v. 8), and he described pursuing Christlikeness as the "one thing I do" (v. 13). The goal of every Christian's life should be to become more like Christ. Despite all the complexity and confusion in the contemporary church, the Christian experience can be summarized by that one great truth. Everything else flows from that. If we are like Christ, we will worship as He worshiped, serve as He served, and relate to others as He did.

The goal of our lives as Christians is outside us. We should not be preoccupied with ourselves but should focus on the Person of Christ to become more like Him. And we can accomplish that only in the power of the Holy Spirit (2 Cor. 3:18).

B. The Barrier of Humanistic Psychology

In the church today, many forces hinder our understanding of that basic truth. Humanistic psychology is one such force. It teaches that man exists for his own satisfaction and has had a devastating effect on Christian theology. According to that philosophy, man must have all his perceived needs and desires met to be happy. Those in the church influenced by that philosophy assume therefore that our goal in life is to meet human needs.

1. Its effect on the gospel

Unfortunately, humanistic philosophy has influenced contemporary presentations of the gospel. Sinners are told only of their value as individuals and of the security and prosperity Jesus can offer them. They are promised health, wealth, and happiness if they will come to Christ.

2. Its effect on sanctification

Contemporary doctrines of sanctification are also fraught with a humanistic mentality. Spiritual growth is often equated with ironing out life's problems and finding personal fulfillment. Much of today's preaching, teaching, and writing is centered on the good of the person rather than the glory of Christ. In his book *Need: The New Religion* (Downer's Grove: InterVarsity, 1985) Tony Walter writes, "It is fashionable to follow the view of some psychologists that the self is a bundle of needs and that personal growth is the business of progressively meeting these needs. Many Christians go along with such beliefs. . . . One mark of the almost total success of this new morality is that the Christian Church, traditionally keen on mortifying the desires of the flesh, on crucifying the needs of the self in pursuit of [Christ's likeness], has eagerly adopted the language of needs for itself. . . . We now hear that 'Jesus will meet your every need,' as though He were some kind of divine psychiatrist or divine detergent, as though God were there simply to serve us" (preface, p. 5).

That kind of mentality leads to a man-centered theology. The satisfaction of our perceived needs becomes the goal of our Christian experience. But that is diametrically opposed to what the Bible teaches. The goal of salvation and sanctification is that we be conformed to the image of Christ (Rom. 8:29). The goal of our lives is not to make sure we're satisfied but to make sure God is satisfied. It's been well said that faith looks out instead of in, and the whole of life falls into line. The more you know Christ and focus on Him, the more the Spirit will make you like Him. But the more you focus on yourself, the more distracted you will be from the proper path.

There's No Secret to Success

I have never met a successful, influential person in any realm of enterprise who was not committed to reaching goals. The people who impact the world are pursuers, competitors, and winners, preoccupied with goals rather than with having their own needs met. All I have learned about the lives of great Christian leaders has made one thing clear: there's no secret to success—they all put out maximum effort to reach spiritual goals and ignore personal satisfaction during the process. It's amazing to discover what great preachers, theologians, and missionaries have suffered in the process of reaching their goals. They were far more concerned with following Christ than with their own condition. Paul counted all things loss and pressed toward the goal of becoming like Christ. That's what made him such a great man.

Being conformed to the image of God's Son is the sum of our Christian duty. That should tremendously simplify the Christian life for us.

Lesson

Philippians 3:17 says to follow godly examples. The next verse says to avoid ungodly ones. That presents a tremendous challenge for the church today. Through the media, bad examples get tremendous exposure. We have to be careful not to follow someone who is masquerading as a friend but is really an enemy of the cross.

I. WARNING ABOUT THE ENEMIES OF THE CROSS (v. 18)

"Many walk, of whom I often told you, and now tell you even weeping, that they are enemies of the cross of Christ."

A. They Are Not Readily Apparent

The implication is that these enemies don't say they are against Christ, His work on the cross, or salvation by grace through faith. Those who openly deny Christ aren't subtle enough to be a threat to the church. They can be spotted immediately. But apparently the people described in this passage say they are friends of Christ, identify with Him, and perhaps are in positions of spiritual leadership. They are a subtle danger, and one needs discernment to recognize them.

Being on guard against hidden enemies is a constant theme in the New Testament. Jesus said, "Beware of the false prophets, who come to you in sheep's clothing, but inwardly are ravenous wolves" (Matt. 7:15). He also predicted that in the last days "many false prophets will arise, and will mislead many" (Matt. 24:11). Throughout the book of Acts we see the apostles dealing with false teachers (cf. 20:28-30). In his letters to Timothy and Titus, Paul warned those ministers many times to teach sound doctrine and avoid anyone who taught contrary to it. Unmasking false teachers is the theme of 2 Peter and Jude. It is also a dominant theme in John's epistles. Throughout Scripture we are reminded to beware of enemies who masquerade as friends.

Unfortunately, many in the church today lack the discernment necessary to flee enemies of the cross. There's a lack of precise biblical teaching and therefore a lack of clear thinking. Many people are victimized by the widespread exposure of those who are actually enemies of the cross.

Paul said, "For many walk," meaning that their daily conduct and pattern of life was against Christ. "Of whom I have often told you" probably refers to the many times Paul had warned the Philippians about false teachers when he was with them. Acts 20:31-32 tells us he warned the Ephesians in a similar way: "Be on the alert, remembering that night and day for a period of three years I did not cease to admonish each one with tears. And now I commend you to God and to the word of His grace, which is able to build you up." Notice we are protected by the Word. If we don't know the Word, we are open to being misled.

B. They Are Cause for Great Concern

In Acts 20 Paul says he warned the Ephesians day and night with tears, and in Romans 9 he talks about being grieved over the lostness of Israel, but Philippians 3:18 is the only record we have of his weeping as he wrote. He was grieved over the encroachment of false teachers who would disrupt the church, lead people astray, and bring reproach upon the name of Christ. Paul was a passionate, tenderhearted man with genuine love for people. He ached over the lost.

He may have been weeping here because the enemies of the cross were lost or because of the terrible impact they would have on the weak members of the church. The Philippian church was special to him because it was the first church in Europe and therefore a beachhead through which a whole new world could be reached. So it was important that the church stay pure and not be misled.

II. DESCRIBING THE ENEMIES OF THE CROSS (v. 19)

"Whose end is destruction, whose god is their appetite, and whose glory is in their shame, who set their minds on earthly things."

Who were the enemies of the cross that Paul was warning the Philippians about? He didn't specifically identify them, so they may have been either Jews or Gentiles.

A. They May Have Been Jews

If they were Jews, we can surmise that in some way they identified with the church and yet remained enemies of the cross. That description fits the Judaizers. They didn't deny Christ or His work on the cross, but they said it was insufficient to bring about salvation. Beyond faith in Christ, they added circumcision and observance of the Mosaic law as requirements for salvation.

The idea that Paul was speaking about the Judaizers fits the context. He was clearly speaking about them in the beginning of the chapter when he said, "Beware of the dogs, beware of the evil workers, beware of the false circumcision" (v. 2). The Judaizers thought they were the sheep, but they were actually the dogs. They thought they were doing good, but they were doing evil. They thought they had the proper circumcision, but Paul said the true circumcision belonged to those "who worship in the Spirit of God and glory in Christ Jesus and put no confidence in the flesh" (v. 3).

When Paul talked about the cross, he referred to the whole of Christ's atoning work and the fact that it alone could provide salvation for sinful men. Paul said, "I determined to know nothing among you except Jesus Christ, and Him crucified" (1 Cor. 2:2). We are saved by the death and resurrection of Christ alone. When we exercise faith in Him, God imputes forgiveness and righteousness to us on that basis alone. But the Judaizers said that wasn't enough.

1. Contemporary parallels

   a) Roman Catholicism

   Roman Catholicism espouses similar doctrine. Official church teaching does not deny the deity or resurrection of Christ or that He died as an atonement for sin. However, it condemns those who believe the sinner is justified by faith in Christ alone, implying we must earn our way to heaven by doing certain works (cf. Council of Trent on justification, canons 9, 24, 30—upheld by Vatican II). That is a heresy not unlike that of the Judaizers.

   b) The Worldwide Church of God

   The Worldwide Church of God, founded by Herbert W. Armstrong, believes many of the facts of the gospel but teaches that obeying the Ten Commandments is necessary for salvation (cf. *The Autobiography of Herbert W. Armstrong*, vol. 1 [Pasadena: Ambassador College, 1967], pp. 281-86). They don't believe the cross is sufficient. They are not friends of the cross but enemies because they add to it. When you add works as a necessity, "grace is no longer grace" (Rom. 11:6).

2. The description as it would relate to the Judaizers

   In Philippians 3:19 Paul describes the enemies of the cross as those "whose end is destruction, whose god is their appetite, and whose glory is in their shame, who set their minds on earthly things." How could that description relate to the Judaizers?

a) Their doom

The end for the Judaizers was destruction because they were not truly saved. The Greek word translated "end" (*telos*) is a reference to one's ultimate destiny. Why was destruction their ultimate destiny? Because trusting in anything beyond Christ is damning.

b) Their deity

"Their god is their appetite" may mean that they worshiped their fleshly accomplishments, which were mostly religious works. It could also refer to their observance of the dietary laws they believed were necessary for salvation.

c) Their disgrace

"Their glory is in their shame" may mean that they were boasting in works they should have been ashamed of. Even the best of accomplishments, outside of what God has wrought, are no better than filthy rags (Isa. 64:6). Paul said he counted all his good deeds apart from Christ as rubbish or manure (Phil. 3:7-8).

d) Their disposition

The Judaizers "set their mind on earthly things" by being preoccupied with ceremonies, feasts, sacrifices, and all kinds of other observances that were merely physical. Colossians 2:17 describes those things as "a mere shadow of what is to come; but the substance belongs to Christ."

Today there are enemies of the cross similar to the Judaizers in that they purport to be orthodox in their doctrine but add works to the gospel. They believe they need to achieve something on their own to be approved by God. We must beware of those who teach that Christ is not sufficient.

B. They May Have Been Gentiles

On the other hand, Paul may have been speaking primarily about Gentiles. In the church there were groups of Gentiles, later known as the Gnostics, who professed Christ but maintained a dualistic philosophy. They believed spirit to be good and matter to be evil. Since the body is matter, they assumed it to be evil no matter what was done with it. But since as Christians we are in the Spirit, they reasoned we didn't have to be concerned about what we do with our bodies. They assumed they could be involved in gluttony, fornication, homosexuality, drunkenness, and other bodily vices without affecting the spirit. The dualism of the Gnostics carried over into what is known in theology as antinomianism.

1. Contemporary parallels

Such disregard for God's standards is manifested today by the person who says, "I'm a Christian. I received Jesus and He changed my spirit, but that doesn't affect how I live. I live as I want." Libertines do exactly the opposite of what the Judaizers did: whereas the Judaizers said, "It's the gospel plus," they say, "It's the gospel minus." They say that when Jesus died He took care of all our sins, so it doesn't matter how we live.

One prominent churchman defended that view in an open letter that said, "I am . . . persuaded that, as [God] did not set his love on me at first for any thing in me, so that love, which is not at all dependent on any thing in me, can never vary on account of my [sins]: and for this reason: when I [sin], suppose by adultery or murder, God ever considers me as one with his own Son, who has fulfilled all righteousness for me." It is true that when we sin we remain in Christ because His righteousness has been imputed to us, but the writer carries that concept much too far: "There are no lengths, then, I may not run, nor any depths I may not fall into, without displeasing [God]. . . . I may murder with [David], worship

Ashtaroth with Solomon, deny Christ with Peter, rob with Onesimus, and commit incest with the Corinthian, without forfeiting either the Divine favour or the kingdom of glory" (cited in *The Works of the Reverend John Fletcher, vol. 1: First Check to Antinomianism* [N.Y.: Carlton & Phillips, 1854], p. 259).

That quotation says we cannot displease God no matter what we do, but that certainly isn't true. It correctly observes that God did not choose us on the basis of who we are but incorrectly assumes it doesn't matter what we become. To the contrary 2 Corinthians 5:17 says, "If any man is in Christ, he is a new creature." Beware of those who say that they believe in Christ but never let it affect their lives.

2. The description as it would relate to the Gnostics

Let's now look at verse 19 from the viewpoint that Paul was speaking about the Gnostics and their antinomian theology.

a) Their doom

The Gnostics' end was destruction because they denied the transforming power of the gospel. They had a useless faith that never brought about a transformation of life (James 2:20).

b) Their deity

Paul said their "god is their appetite." The Greek word translated "appetite" is *koilia*, from which we get the word *colitis*. It refers to the mid-section—particularly the stomach. That would clearly apply to the Gnostics since they were driven by sensual desires. False leaders often say they are friends of the cross but espouse a gospel that does not include virtue or holiness. Rather, they are motivated by their fleshly appetites.

c) Their disgrace

"Whose glory is in their shame" means they boasted about things they should have been ashamed of. That's reminiscent of the Corinthian church. It was bad enough that a man among them was engaging in incest, but what was worse was that the church was actually boasting about it (1 Cor. 5:1-6)! While the Judaizer boasts of his self-effort, the libertine boasts of his sin. He says, "I'm saved; I'm covered by the blood—it doesn't matter what I do." They abuse the concept of Christian liberty to defend the shameful things they do (1 Cor. 6:12).

d) Their disposition

Verse 19 concludes, "[They] set their minds on earthly things." The Judaizers were into earthly ceremonies and rituals that were mere symbols, but the libertines loved the world itself. James 4:4 says, "Do you not know that friendship with the world is hostility toward God? Therefore whoever wishes to be a friend of the world makes himself an enemy of God." First John 2:15 says, "If anyone loves the world, the love of the Father is not in him." Such a person is afflicted with what Paul Rees termed "thing-mindedness" (*The Adequate Man: Paul in Philippians* [Revell, 1959], p. 90). He's like the man at the Interpreter's house in the second part of *The Pilgrim's Progress* with muckrake in hand, eyes continually focused downward on the things of this world. He ignored the celestial being above him offering a heavenly crown for his muckrake. Like him, some leaders in the church today are obsessed with houses, cars, bank accounts, trips, wardrobes, and other worldly things.

To effectively pursue the prize, we need not only to follow the right examples but to avoid the wrong ones. We must be able to discern who the enemies of the cross are by examining their doctrine and their lives. They may add to the gospel by saying we need to earn our salvation or subtract from it by saying it doesn't matter how we live. Listening to them will only turn us away from the path of Christlikeness.

Focusing on the Facts

1. What should be the goal of every Christian's life (see p. 30)?
2. How has humanistic psychology influenced gospel presentations (see pp. 30-31)?
3. What is much of today's preaching, teaching, and writing centered on (see p. 31)?
4. What did all the great preachers, theologians, and missionaries have in common (see p. 32)?
5. What is implied about the enemies of the cross in Philippians 3:18-19 (see p. 32)?
6. What are two possible reasons Paul is weeping when he writes verses 18-19 (see p. 34)?
7. What did the Judaizers add to faith in Christ as requirements for salvation (see p. 34)?
8. What did Paul refer to when he talked about the cross (see p. 35)?
9. Name two contemporary parallels to the heresy of the Judaizers (see p. 35).
10. In what way did the Judaizers "set their mind on earthly things" (Phil. 3:19; see p. 36)?
11. Describe the attitude of contemporary libertines toward sin (see p. 37).
12. What is one verse that refutes the idea that God didn't choose us on the basis of who we are so it doesn't matter what we become (see p. 38)?
13. While the Judaizer boasts in his self-effort, the libertine boasts in his _____. Explain (see p. 39).

Pondering the Principles

1. Will Metzger's book *Tell the Truth* (Downers Grove: InterVarsity, 1984) contrasts a man-centered gospel with a God-centered gospel (pp. 32-33). Here are some of the things it points out:

A Man-centered Gospel	A God-centered Gospel
Point of contact with non-Christians is love. (God loves you.) Therefore, God's authority is secondary.	Point of contact with non-Christians is creation. (God made you.) Therefore, God has authority over your destiny.
Christ exists for our benefit.	Christ exists to gather a kingdom and receive honor and glory.
Man seeks the truth but lacks the correct facts.	Man's mind is at enmity with God; no one seeks God apart from divine intervention.
Man is to give mental assent to the truths of the gospel—emphasis on decision.	Man is to respond with his whole being (mind, heart, and will)—emphasis on conversion.

Evaluate how you share the gospel, and make any needed changes the next time you have the opportunity to speak of Christ.

2. Look at Matthew 23:2-10. There Jesus described false teachers in a way that helps us identify them. First, they lack real authority, although they claim to speak for God (v. 2). Second, they lack integrity because they do not practice what they preach (v. 3). Third, they lack sympathy because they burden people with legalistic demands while showing little tenderness or concern for them (v. 4). Fourth, they lack true spirituality because they put on an outward show to receive praise from men (v. 5). And fifth, they lack humility because their focus is on the privileges their position brings them (vv. 6-7).

3. James Boice said this about the Gnostics in his commentary on *The Epistles of John* (Grand Rapids: Zondervan, 1979): "They claimed to know God; but even as they made their claims they showed by their actions that they failed to take sin, which is opposed to the nature of God, seriously. Their religion consisted from the ethical standpoint of what Dietrich Bonhoeffer called 'easy grace.' They claimed fellowship with God, but the fellowship was not costly. They separated religion and ethics. Conse-

quently, they claimed the highest privileges while living precisely as they pleased." John's first epistle was written primarily to combat the teaching of the Gnostics. Read it with that in mind, making sure that no false doctrine has affected your views of sin and salvation.

4
Focusing on Expectations

Outline

Introduction and Review

Lesson
I. The Expectation of Heaven (v. 20*a*)
  A. It Is Our Hope
    1. Paul's preoccupation with heaven
    2. The contemporary church's preoccupation
      with the world
  B. It Is Our Home
II. The Expectation of Christ's Return (v. 20*b*)
  A. It Provides Motivation
  B. It Provides Accountability
  C. It Provides Security
III. The Expectation of a New Body (v. 21)
  A. When Will Christ Transform Our Bodies?
  B. How Will Christ Transform Our Bodies?
  C. Why Will Christ Transform Our Bodies?

Conclusion

Introduction and Review

We have been studying Philippians 3:12-21. The key verse is verse 14, where Paul says, "I press on toward the goal for the prize of the upward call of God in Christ Jesus." The prize he was reaching for was to be like Christ. That pursuit is the basic duty of every believer.

However, our society is not conducive to our becoming like Christ. Ours is what has been called a sensate culture because most people are more concerned with pleasant emotions than with productive efforts—they're more into comfort than accomplishment. They're moving fast toward nothing, having no other goals than personal comfort and freedom from responsibility. And that has affected even the church, which suffers from an appalling apathy. We have forgotten that we are soldiers in a holy war. Ephesians 6:14 says to "stand firm . . . having girded your loins with truth." The first thing a soldier put on when he went to battle was a sash or a belt around his waist. He would tie it as tight as he could and pull the corners of his tunic up through the belt, so that he could have complete freedom of movement in hand-to-hand combat. The belt of truthfulness is not a piece of armor for it can't protect us directly, nor is it a weapon. But it does indicate that we are serious about the battle and devoted to achieving victory.

In Philippians 3:17-21 we find some necessary elements to achieving victory in our pursuit of Christlikeness. The first is following godly examples (v. 17; see pp. 23-27), and the second is fleeing from enemies (vv. 18-19; see pp. 32-40).

Lesson

The final element in reaching for the prize is focusing on expectations. Verses 20-21 say, "Our citizenship is in heaven, from which also we eagerly wait for a Savior, the Lord Jesus Christ; who will transform the body of our humble state into conformity with the body of His glory, by the exertion of the power that He has even to subject all things to Himself." We are to look forward to hearing the words "well done" from the Savior and receiving our reward from Him.

I. THE EXPECTATION OF HEAVEN (v. 20*a*)

"Our citizenship is in heaven."

We must have a heavenly perspective as we pursue the prize of Christlikeness.

A. It Is Our Hope

1. Paul's preoccupation with heaven

The apostle Paul was preoccupied with heaven; he knew few earthly comforts. He was beaten, stoned, left for dead, deprived of necessities, and frequently disappointed by people. He often experienced pain and sorrow. But he had no concern for pleasant feelings: he wanted only to live a productive life in pursuit of his heavenly goal. That's why he had "the desire to depart and be with Christ, for that is very much better" (Phil. 1:23).

We must have the same focus if we are going to pursue Christlikeness. Christ is from heaven and in heaven. Heaven is His place, and because we are His, heaven is our place as well. If we're preoccupied with being like Him, we'll naturally be preoccupied with heaven. What happens there should be more important to us than what happens here. So verse 20 says, "Our citizenship is in heaven, from which also we eagerly wait for a Savior, the Lord Jesus Christ."

The time is coming when we will be "caught up . . . to meet the Lord in the air, and thus we shall always be with the Lord" (1 Thess. 4:17). In verse 14 of our text Paul called that "the upward call of God in Christ Jesus." He longed for that glorious moment personally. But he knew his time on earth was important because he had a ministry to complete (Phil. 1:23-24). As he came to the end of his task he looked forward to being with his Savior in heaven even more, saying in 2 Timothy 4:7-8, "I have fought the good fight, I have finished the course, I have kept the faith; in the future there is laid up for me the crown of righteousness, which the Lord, the righteous Judge, will award to me on that day; and not only to me, but also to all who have loved his appearing."

2. The contemporary church's preoccupation with the world

Paul's longing for a better place than this earth is strange to many of us in the contemporary church. Leaving this earth and going to heaven is not a popular thought. Our increasing emphasis on success, prosperity, and personal problem-solving reflects our earth-bound perspective. This world has become our place. We need to be reminded that Jesus said, "Do not lay up for yourselves treasures upon earth, where moth and rust destroy, and where thieves break in and steal" (Matt. 6:19).

It's also hard for us to comprehend a future heavenly reward. In our materialistic age we rarely experience delayed gratification. Almost whatever we want, we can have immediately. We don't even have to have money —we can use a credit card. We don't have to build any-thing—we can buy it. And we don't have to go very far to get it. So a heavenly reward may not seem quite as interesting because we have to wait for it.

Our lack of interest in heaven is the other side of our preoccupation with this world. Heaven is practically ignored by modern evangelicals. There is little preaching or teaching on the subject, but we do hear mammoth amounts of material on how we can prosper in this life. If we are going to pursue Christlikeness with the same passion as Paul, we must get our focus off this world and on the world to come.

B. It Is Our Home

Paul says "our citizenship is in heaven." We are not citizens of this world. The Greek word translated "citizenship" is used only here and refers to a colony of foreigners. In a secular source it is used to describe a capital city that kept the names of its citizens on a register. Indeed, we are registered citizens of another place—heaven. Our names are there, our Father is there, our brothers and sisters are there, and our inheritance is there—it is our home.

The Philippians understood what Paul was saying because they were a colony of Roman citizens far from Rome. Another example is the Israelites during the Babylonian Captivity. Many of them, however, had become so entrenched in Babylonian culture that they didn't want to leave when it came time to return to the Promised Land. That seems analogous to many of us in the church. When the Lord says it's time to go to heaven, we fight it as if it were the worst thing imaginable because this world has become everything to us. But we must understand that our citizenship is in heaven.

II. THE EXPECTATION OF CHRIST'S RETURN (v. 20*b*)

"From which also we eagerly wait for a Savior, the Lord Jesus Christ."

Our Lord is in heaven, and He will soon come to take us there. Jesus said, "In my Father's house are many dwelling places. . . . I go to prepare a place for you. . . . I will come again, and receive you to Myself; that where I am, there you may be also" (John 14:2-3). We are not waiting for an event as much as we are waiting for a Person.

Do You Want to Go Through the Tribulation?

Until about ten years ago, most of the evangelical church believed strongly in a pre-Tribulation rapture—that the next event on the prophetic calendar is Jesus' coming to escort the church into heaven (1 Thess. 4:16-17). Then on earth would follow the seven-year period known as the Great Tribulation, after which the Lord would return with His saints to set up a literal kingdom. But recently the view that the church will go through the Tribulation and be raptured at the end has become more popular. And I don't think that's happened primarily because of exegetical or theological reasons; I believe the shift may be a reflection of a subconscious preoccupation with this world. Perhaps many of us would like to see all those things we've read about in the book of Revelation. Maybe we're so much a part of this world that we'd like to see how the whole thing

47

ends. Revelation is the preview of coming attractions, so it is possible that we don't want to miss the main feature.

That's not the only valid reason for the popularity of the post-Tribulational view, but I do believe there is an unhealthy preoccupation with those upcoming events and an indifference about being with Christ. I'm not waiting for the Antichrist; I'm waiting for Christ Himself!

Romans 8:23 says we as Christians "groan within ourselves, waiting eagerly for our adoption as sons, the redemption of our body." Why? Because "the sufferings of this present time are not worthy to be compared with the glory that is to be revealed to us" (v. 18). Peter said that the earth will eventually be burned up. Therefore he said, "Since all these things are to be destroyed in this way, what sort of people ought you to be in holy conduct and godliness, looking for and hastening the coming of the day of God" (2 Pet. 3:11-12). First John 3:2-3 says, "When He appears, we shall be like Him, because we shall see Him just as He is. And everyone who has this hope fixed on Him purifies himself."

Anticipating Christ's coming is the greatest source of spiritual motivation, accountability, and security.

A. It Provides Motivation

Knowing that Jesus is coming provides tremendous motivation in our reaching for the prize because we'll want to be ready when He comes. We'll want to have been faithful in serving Him. First Corinthians 3:13-14 says, "Each man's work will become evident; for the day will show it, because it is to be revealed with fire; and the fire itself will test the quality of each man's work. If any man's work which he has built upon it remains, he shall receive a reward." We find motivation in the hope of one day being rewarded by Christ and hearing, "Well done, good and faithful slave. . . . Enter into the joy of your master" (Matt. 25:23).

B. It Provides Accountability

Second John 8 says, "Watch yourselves, that you might not lose what we have accomplished, but that you may receive a full reward." We know that "each one of us shall give an account of himself to God" (Rom. 14:12) and that "if any man's work is burned up, he shall suffer loss" (1 Cor. 3:15). That accountability should keep us pursuing the prize. First Corinthians 4:5 says that when the Lord comes, He will "bring to light the things hidden in the darkness and disclose the motives of men's hearts."

C. It Provides Security

In John 14:3 Jesus says, "I will come again." Acts 1:11 says, "This Jesus, who has been taken up from you into heaven, will come in just the same way as you have watched Him go into heaven." In John 6:39 Jesus says, "This is the will of Him who sent Me, that of all He has given Me I lose nothing, but raise it up on the last day."

As we think about the return of Christ and the promise of being with Him, we gain motivation, accountability, and security. What happens in this world doesn't matter nearly as much. Why? Because we know we have "an inheritance which is imperishable and undefiled and will not fade away, reserved in heaven" (1 Pet. 1:4).

Presently we don't live in heaven physically, but in a sense we do live in the heavenly realm. Ephesians 1:3 says, "Blessed be the God and Father of our Lord Jesus Christ, who has blessed us with every spiritual blessing in the heavenly places." Though we are not in heaven, we are experiencing heavenly life. We have the life of God within us. We are under the rule of a heavenly King, and we obey heaven's laws. So we experience "a foretaste of glory divine," as Fanny Crosby noted in the hymn "Blessed Assurance." We are living in a new community, enjoying a new fellowship that will fully come to fruition in a place called heaven.

We're to "eagerly await" Christ's return (Phil. 3:20). The Greek verb used is found in most passages dealing with the second coming and expresses the idea of waiting patiently but with great anticipation.

The Place Where We'll Spend Eternity

Where is heaven? The only thing the Bible says about the location of heaven is that it's up. In Revelation 4:1 John is told from heaven, "Come up here." Second Corinthians 12:2 calls it "the third heaven." The first heaven is the atmosphere, the second the universe, and the third heaven beyond that. The moon is more than 200,000 miles away, and that's the closest celestial body to us. The star called Betelgeuse is said to be 270 light-years from earth. And that is close, relatively speaking—there are far more stars and galaxies beyond that. So heaven is far away, but it doesn't take long to get there. Jesus said to the thief on the cross, "*Today* you shall be with Me in Paradise" (Luke 23:43, emphasis added). Second Corinthians 5:8 says, "To be absent from the body [is] to be at home with the Lord."

What is heaven like? Ezekiel 1 describes it, but its description is hard to understand. That's because we cannot fully comprehend the beauty and magnificence of our eternal home. Revelation 21 and 22 make a little more sense. We read about jewels, light, gold, angels, a temple, and the presence of God. We read about the absence of tears, pain, and death. Everything is perfect. The angels and the redeemed from all the ages of history are there. It has a capital city called the New Jerusalem, which is made of pure gold and has twelve great gates made of pearl. In that description we get a glimpse of the majesty of heaven, but it really is indescribable. It's beyond the mind's ability to grasp.

So we "eagerly wait for a Savior, the Lord Jesus Christ" (Phil. 3:20). Our anticipation is not of an event, but of a Person. The goal we pursue during our lives is to be like Christ, and the prize is that we will be made like Him when He returns (1 John 3:3).

III. THE EXPECTATION OF A NEW BODY (v. 21)

"[Christ] will transform the body of our humble state into conformity with the body of His glory."

We look forward to His coming because we desire to be transformed. As we noted in Romans 8:23, we long to be free from our sinful flesh and be perfect like Christ. We have been made a new creation in the inner man, but that inner man is incarcerated in unredeemed flesh. Our fallen humanness and its lusts remain with us. The new creation within us longs to be liberated from the sin that remains. Paul said, "Who will set me free from the body of this death? Thanks be to God through Jesus Christ our Lord!" (Rom. 7:24-25). So we long for Christ to come and "transform the body of our humble state."

A. When Will Christ Transform Our Bodies?

If we die any time before Christ comes for His own, our bodies go into the grave. Our spirits, however, immediately go to be with the Lord (2 Cor. 5:8; Phil. 1:23). We join the "spirits of righteous men made perfect" (Heb. 12:23). Our bodies, however, will await the second coming of Christ. At that time He will raise them all (1 Thess. 4:16) and transform them.

B. How Will Christ Transform Our Bodies?

The Greek word translated "transformed" is *metaschēmatizō*, from which we get the word *schematic*. A schematic is simply an internal design of something. So God will redesign and refashion our bodies into ones adapted to an eternal, holy heaven. We will then be like Christ was after His resurrection. He ate, talked, and walked like other men but also appeared and disappeared, flying through space from earth to heaven at will. He was recognizable as a man but was also transcendent.

First Corinthians 15:42-43 says this about our resurrection body: "It is sown a perishable body, it is raised an imperishable body; it is sown in dishonor, it is raised in glory; it is sown in weakness, it is raised in power." So in heaven we will have a perfect spirit and a perfect form, which will combine to perfectly manifest the glory of God. Everything that inhibits us from doing what God wants will be eliminated. We will be free from all evil. There will be no sin, sorrow, pain, disappointment, doubt, fear, temptation, weakness, failure, hate, anger, quarrels, repentance, or confession. There will be perfect comfort, pleasure, knowledge, love, and joy.

Paul says we will be transformed "into conformity with the body of His glory" (Phil. 3:21). First John 3:2 says, "When He appears, we shall be like Him, because we shall see Him just as He is." Not only has God saved us from hell and given us heaven, but He will also make us like His Son—all a product of His magnanimous grace. The Greek word translated "conformed" is the same word used in Romans 8:29, which says God's goal in saving us is that we might "become conformed to the image of His Son."

C. Why Will Christ Transform Our Bodies?

When we die, our spirits are instantly perfected. When Christ returns, our bodies are raised and transformed to be like Christ as holy instruments for worship and service. We will never again have an evil impulse or an errant motive. Our minds and hearts will be filled with the pure light of God's truth and undiluted love, joy, peace, and goodness. Our emotions will be allowed their full expression, but they will always be in perfect balance. We ought to long for that with all our hearts.

Conclusion

The end of Philippians 3 assures us that Christ has the power to do the marvelous things He has promised "by the exertion of the power that He has even to subject all things to Himself." Since Christ can subject the entire universe to His sovereign control, He certainly has enough power to raise our bodies and make us like Him. The word translated "subject" speaks of arranging things in order of rank or managing something. Our Lord has the power to providentially create natural laws and to miraculously overrule them. He has the power to give life and to take it. First Corinthians 15:23-27 says, "At His coming, then comes the end, when He delivers up the kingdom to the God and Father, when He has abolished all rule and all authority and power. For He must reign until He has put all His enemies under His feet. . . . For He has put all things in subjection under His feet." The same power that will recapture the entire fallen universe and give it back to God is what makes it possible for us to become like Christ.

So by placing our hope in the second coming of Christ we find motivation, accountability, and security. Where is your focus? I hope it is on heaven and that you have not been distracted.

Phocas, the Heavenly Minded Martyr

Paul Rees recounts the story of Phocas, known as the Gardener Saint of Asia Minor:

"Belonging to the fourth century, he lived in a little cottage outside the city gate of Sinope. Travellers passed his door almost all hours of the day and night. By the holy ingenuity of love he stopped as many of them as possible. Were they not weary? Let them rest themselves, sitting in his well-tended garden. Were they in need of a friendly word? He would speak it to them—in the dear Master's name.

"But then, quite suddenly one day, life was all changed for Phocas. Orders went out from Emperor Diocletian that the Christians must be put [to death]. When the persecutors entered Sinope, they were under orders to find a man by the name of Phocas and put him to death. About to enter the city one hot afternoon, they passed in front of the old man's cottage and garden. In his innocence he treated them as though they were his warmest friends, begging them to pause a while and rest themselves. They consented. So warm and gracious was the hospitality they received that when their host invited them to stay the night and go on their way refreshed next day, they agreed to do so.

"'And what is your business?' said Phocas, unsuspectingly. They then told him that they would answer his question if he would regard it as a secret. It was obvious to them by now that he was a man to be trusted. Who were they? Why, they were the lictors of

Rome, searching for a certain 'Phocas,' who was a Christian. And please, if their kind host knew him would he be so good as to help them to identify him. After all, he was a dangerous follower of this Jesus about whom the Christians talked, and he must be executed immediately.

"'I know him well,' said Phocas quietly. 'He is quite near. . . . Let us attend to it in the morning.'

"His guests having retired, Phocas sat thinking. Escape? That would be easy. He had only to leave under cover of darkness. At daybreak he could be at least twenty miles away. He knew fellow Christians who would give him hospitality by hiding him. When the persecution had passed, he could reappear and once again cultivate his garden.

"The decision to flee into safety or stay unto death was apparently made without struggle or delay. Out into his garden Phocas went and began digging. Was there any earthly thing he loved better than this little plot of ground—the odour of the humus, the 'feel' of the soil, the miracle of fertility. What were his thoughts as he went on digging?

"There was still time to run away. But the Saviour did not run— neither from His Gethsemane nor His Calvary. Or, perhaps he thought of his fellow Christians to whom he might go for asylum. Would not his coming endanger them? As for these executioners that now were soundly sleeping under his roof, they were, after all, only men who were carrying out orders. If they failed to find their man, their own lives, likely as not, would be taken.

"Deeper and deeper Phocas dug. Before dawn he was done. There it was—his own grave.

"Morning came, and with it the waking of the executioners. 'I am Phocas,' he said calmly. We have it on the word of the Christian bishop who recorded the story for posterity, that the men stood 'motionless' in astonishment. They couldn't believe it! And when they did believe it, they obviously were reluctant to perform an execution without mercy on a man who had shown them nothing but mercy.

"It was the persuasion of Phocas himself that overcame their reluctance. They had a duty to perform. He knew it. He was not bitter at them. Besides, death did not terrify him, he assured them. Toward them he bore nothing but the love of Christ.

"Moments later it was all over. The sword had done its work. And the body of Christ's love-mastered man lay in the stillness of death in the garden he loved so dearly" (*Prayer and Life's Highest* [Grand Rapids: Eerdmans, 1956], pp. 47-49).

The hope of heaven removes fear. May we focus on that hope as we reach for the prize of Christlikeness.

Focusing on the Facts

1. Many people in our culture are more into _____ than _____ (see p. 44).
2. What does the belt of truth signify in Ephesians 6:14 (see p. 44)?
3. We must have a _____ perspective as we pursue the prize of Christlikeness (see p. 45).
4. Paul longed for the time he would be with Christ, yet what did he know about his time on earth and why (Phil. 1:23-24; see p. 45)?
5. Why is it hard for many of us in the contemporary church to relate to future reward (see p. 46)?
6. What is the other side of our preoccupation with this world (see p. 46)?
7. What does the Greek word translated "citizenship" refer to (see p. 47)?
8. What view of future events has become popular in recent years (see p. 47)?
9. What three things does the hope of Christ's coming provide for the believer (see pp. 48-49)?
10. In what sense do we presently live in the heavenly realm (see p. 49)?
11. Where is heaven? What is it like (see p. 50)?
12. Where do our spirits go when we die? What's the fate of our bodies (see p. 51)?
13. What was Christ like when He appeared on earth after His resurrection (see p. 51)?
14. Describe the sovereign power of Christ (Phil. 3:21; see pp. 52-53).
15. The hope of heaven removes _____ (see p. 55).

Pondering the Principles

1. According to Jesus Christ, the hope of heaven is reserved only for those who obey Him regardless of the cost: "Not everyone who says to Me, 'Lord, Lord,' will enter the kingdom of heaven; but he who does the will of My Father who is in heaven" (Matt. 7:21). "The kingdom of heaven is like a treasure hidden in the field, which a man found and hid; and from joy over it he goes and sells all that he has, and buys that field" (Matt. 13:44). Recognize the surpassing value of Christ above every earthly thing, and reflect that attitude by how you live and what you focus on.

2. In Matthew 24:42 Jesus says, "Be on the alert, for you do not know which day your Lord is coming." C. S. Lewis wrote, "Precisely because we cannot predict the moment, we must be ready at all moments. Our Lord repeated this practical conclusion again and again; as if the promise of the Return had been made for the sake of this conclusion alone. Watch, watch, is the burden of His advice. I shall come like a thief. You will not, I most solemnly assure you, you will not see me approaching. If the householder had known at which time the burglar would arrive, he would have been ready for him. If the servant had known when his absent employer would come home, he wouldn't have been found drunk in the kitchen. But they didn't. Nor will you. Therefore you must be ready at all times" (*The Inspirational Writings of C. S. Lewis* [New York: Inspirational Press, 1987], p. 371).

Scripture Index

Topical Index